A SELF-DEVELOPMENT PROGRAMME
Telephonetechniques

Acknowledgments

When I was first asked to write this book by Chris Roebuck, I
didn't think it would be possible. Although I have been training
telephone techniques programmes for many years, it's totally
different to write it all on paper. Research says that to stand in front
of a group of people and train them, to some people is more
frightening than death itself. To me writing a book makes me feel
the same.

Please give me a live audience next time, not a wordprocessor.
I would like to thank all of the people who had faith in me,
especially my husband and best friend David, who has given
me much support and many hours of his time, trying to
unravel some of my more ambitious thoughts into some sort
of tangible reality. Thanks also to my two children, Jordan and
Charis who gave me lots of space in order to finish the book.
Special thanks must also go to my friends and colleagues:
Alison Naisby, Liz Brown of Sorbus Training and Susan
Hilland of Corporate Training plc., for their many ideas and
material help with the content of this book.

A SELF-DEVELOPMENT PROGRAMME

Telephone techniques

THE ESSENTIAL GUIDE TO THINKING AND WORKING SMARTER

Lin Walker

MARSHALL PUBLISHING • LONDON

A Marshall Edition
Conceived, edited and
designed by
Marshall Editions Ltd
The Orangery
161 New Bond Street
London W1Y 9PA

First published in the UK
in 1998 by
Marshall Publishing Ltd

Copyright © 1998
Marshall Editions
Developments Ltd

ISBN 1-84028-132-4

Series Consultant Editor
Chris Roebuck
Project Editor Jo Wells
at Axis Design
Designer Martin Laurie
at Axis Design
Indexer Livia Vass
at Axis Design

Art Director Sean Keogh
Managing Editor
Clare Currie
Editorial Assistant
Sophie Sandy
Editorial Coordinator
Becca Clunes
Production Nikki Ingram
Jacket Design
Poppy Jenkins

Originated in Italy by
Articolor
Printed and bound in
France by SIRC

Video Arts quotes extracted from training films:
pp15, 20, 28, 42, 66: "Telephone Behaviour"

Contents

1

Communication
First impressions
Interruptions
Common pitfalls

How much do you rely on the telephone?

Does the telephone interrupt your work?

Have you had any telephone training?

How Do You Use The Telephone?

This book is about:

■ developing a
professional approach

■ understanding the
pitfalls

■ responding to
questions and queries

■ taking messages

■ transferring calls

■ dealing with difficult
calls

■ creating a good
environment for
communication

The telephone is one of the most used but least understood of business tools. It enables you to communicate with people over large distances, saving you time and money – at least it should!

Just stop and think for a moment about how much of your working day is spent using the telephone. How much of your company or organization's business relies on the telephone? For some businesses, such as mail order companies or help desks, the telephone is almost their entire source of revenue.

How reliant are you personally on the telephone to enable you to do your job? If you run your own business you may depend on the telephone for orders and to get in touch with your suppliers or sub-contractors. Imagine being without a telephone. How would it affect your working day?

The negative side

The problem with the telephone, however, is that it often rings when you are busy and don't really want to be disturbed. Except for telephones with modern caller number display panels, the phone often doesn't allow you to see who is calling, so you may end up talking to someone who you would not choose to talk to at that precise moment. Telephone calls can be a time-consuming, troublesome intrusion into

your busy life, yet try being in business without a telephone!

Be aware of the power of the telephone – it creates opportunities and conveys information in a fast and effective way, but unless it is managed properly it makes you instantly available to other people at any time of the day.

Like millions of people in the modern business world, you are probably expected to use the telephone on a daily basis, and yet you have never been trained in how to use it effectively. You may say: "But what is there to know about using the telephone? It rings, you pick up the receiver and speak. When the conversation is over you replace the receiver and that's all there is to it." If only it were that easy.

Telephones are such a regular feature of our everyday lives, it is easy to take them for granted and assume we know how to use them to good effect. Yet there are numerous pitfalls of telephone communication.

First impressions last

The caller receives an impression within the first few seconds of the telephone being answered and that impression is essential to the future relationship that you have with either the individual or their organization. So it is crucial to get it right and make sure that the first impression is a positive one.

DO ANY OF THESE STATEMENTS RING TRUE?
Write your thoughts in the space provided.

Using the telephone is easy.

_____
_____
_____
_____

I communicate well over the telephone, the problem is other people.

_____
_____
_____
_____

Why can't callers work out what they want BEFORE they call me?

_____
_____
_____
_____

If that telephone rings one more time I'll scream!

_____
_____
_____
_____

Why are some people so rude over the telephone?

_____
_____
_____
_____

When you get to the end of the book, turn back to this page and review your thoughts again and see where and how your views have changed.

The first few seconds of a call will create a lasting impression.

Weighing Up The Pros And Cons

The telephone is the "front door", and the way you open that door indicates the way you will handle your contacts in the future.

Whenever you speak to a stranger on the telephone your perception of them is determined solely by what you hear through the earpiece. Similarly, whenever you talk to someone on the telephone their perception of you is also determined solely by what they hear.

The telephone can be the first or only communication that you have with a customer or business contact. It is a very powerful tool and it is essential for your business that it is used effectively. The telephone provides you with the means to communicate what your service is really about, how competent you are as an individual, and how effective and efficient your organization is.

Have you ever said, "I'm a really good judge of character, I know immediately if I'm going to get on with someone", or, "I don't like their approach I'll never be able to do business with them". What are you basing your assumptions on? In all likelihood you are basing your opinion on a simple matter of behaviour – how the caller sounds. If someone answers the telephone using an inappropriate tone – perhaps a little abrupt or annoyed, or laughing and joking – it could easily create the wrong first impression.

The image you project on the telephone, and the initial rapport you create with the caller is extremely important. The questions you ask and the way you respond will show what sort of person you are and what kind of organization you represent.

Barriers to effective telephone use

When you are dealing with someone face-to-face you can pick up a good deal of information very quickly. You can see what the person looks like, how they are dressed, how old they are, what their facial expressions are, and what their body language is "saying".

At the same time as you are picking up all of this information about the person who you are talking to they can pick up the same information about you. Both of you then react accordingly.

But when you are communicating with someone over the telephone you do not have all of this "extra" information and as a result you may encounter problems. Think through the potential problems that may arise when you are using the telephone and why they might occur. Perhaps you work in a very noisy and distracting open-plan office, or you feel embarrassed when talking to people on the telephone.

Be aware of the benefits

Think about the benefits that using the telephone has for you personally. To help you get started some of the benefits are listed opposite, but try to draw on specific examples from your own life.

PROBLEMS WITH THE TELEPHONE

■ It is more difficult to establish rapport because of the absence of body language in your conversation. Body language is a major element in face-to-face communication.

■ You can accidentally intrude on someone at an inconvenient time. This is particularly likely if you make the call to a mobile telephone.

■ There is more chance that either party will jump to the wrong conclusions than if you were engaged in face-to-face communication.

■ On the telephone you are prone to distractions.

■ It is more difficult to communicate complicated information and ideas accurately.

"You never get a second chance to create a first impression."
Dale Carnegie

BENEFITS THAT THE TELEPHONE BRINGS TO YOU

■ It is often easier to gain access to the person who you want to speak to over the telephone than in person.

■ It is quick, easy and convenient. The telephone is sitting on your desk. Instead of having to arrange an appointment, you can approach the person you need to, find out the information you require and be able to conclude the matter in the shortest possible time.

■ Telephone conversations are normally shorter than face-to-face interactions, so you can achieve more in a given amount of time.

■ Telephone conversations are usually confined to you and one other person, so it is easier to take control of the conversation.

■ The telephone is a great equalizer. It is therefore relatively easy for younger people to sound more authoritative on the telephone.

2

Questions
Scores
Statements
Assessment

How do you perform?

Are you good at taking messages?

How well do you listen?

How Well Do You Perform?

Because telephones are an everyday part of life, you probably never consider whether your telephone "performance" is good or bad. Most people believe that their telephone skills are fairly good, purely because of the familiarity of the machine. But does practice really make perfect? Just because you have had years of experience using the telephone does not mean that you know how to use it effectively. And when problems arise most people tend to blame the person on the other end of the telephone.

To start to build up a realistic picture of how well you are performing, answer the questionnaires in this chapter. Your answers should help you to find out just

BE BRUTALLY HONEST WITH YOURSELF – HAVE YOU EVER DONE ANY OF THE FOLLOWING?

- misunderstood someone over the telephone

- wished you were talking to the other person face-to-face

- felt frustrated with the person at the other end of the telephone

- wanted to "strangle" the other person

- felt that the person at the other end of the line is uncooperative

- blamed the person on the other end of the line when they did not understand you

- decided that you don't like someone because of their voice

- lost the thread of a conversation

- been unhelpful because you were busy

If you have said yes to any of the above, then your performance over the telephone may not be as good as you would like to believe.

how good you really are. Try to answer each questionnaire fairly quickly, without stopping to think too hard about your answers. This will help you to be more honest with yourself. And the more open and honest you are able to be, the more benefit you will get from the results in the end.

Even though you may already be a good communicator on the telephone, you can always be better. This is your opportunity to see how well you are doing at the moment and to improve your skills where required. You can find out how you are doing in all the major areas where you use the telephone at work. The following chapters will help you to put together a plan to develop your skills. Use the self-assessments, ideas and checklists in order to regularly assess how your skills have developed and to help you in the future.

The way you will improve your skills is by using simple formats that you can transfer effectively to work. Building up an understanding of how telephone communication works will allow you to be effective in situations that may not be covered by this book.

The most effective way of improving is to assess your skills, which are based on previous experiences, identify and improve on your areas of weakness and capitalize on your strengths. This will allow you to target the time and effort that you put into developing your skills, concentrating on where it is really needed and where it will bring the most benefit. This process will accustom you to taking control of your own development. Do not assume that your organization will take care of your development, many do not. Be aware of your own needs so that if the organization does not develop you fully you can plan your own improvement.

..To the caller, the person answering the call is the organisation...

Receiving A Telephone Call

How you answer the telephone can mean the difference between meeting your monthly performance targets and losing an important sale, or between a promotion and being passed over again. So it is worth getting it right.

Many of us pick up bad habits without realizing it, or are held back from improving our performance by ideas which have become ingrained and affect the way we do our jobs. By assessing yourself you will highlight just such ideas and areas where your performance could do with either a complete overhaul or a quick brush up.

Read each question carefully, then tick the answer that you feel best describes how you behave. Be as honest and objective as you can.

Put a circle around each of your scores, work out your final score and check how well you did.

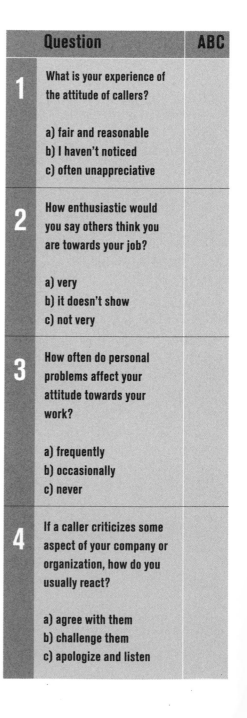

Question	ABC
1 What is your experience of the attitude of callers? a) fair and reasonable b) I haven't noticed c) often unappreciative	
2 How enthusiastic would you say others think you are towards your job? a) very b) it doesn't show c) not very	
3 How often do personal problems affect your attitude towards your work? a) frequently b) occasionally c) never	
4 If a caller criticizes some aspect of your company or organization, how do you usually react? a) agree with them b) challenge them c) apologize and listen	

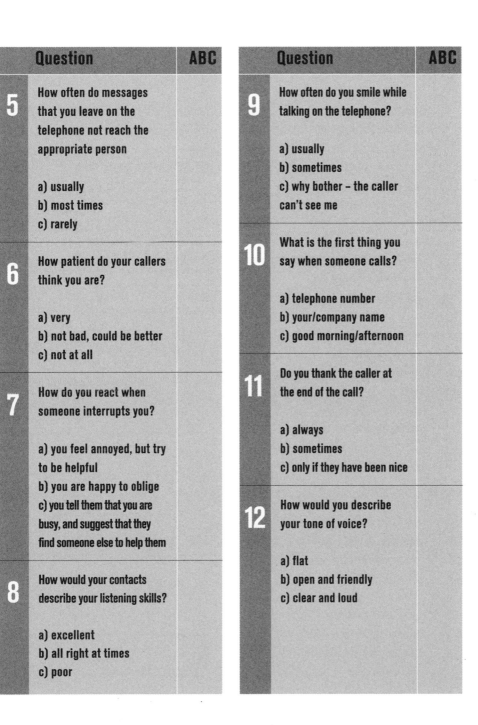

	Question	ABC
5	How often do messages that you leave on the telephone not reach the appropriate person a) usually b) most times c) rarely	
6	How patient do your callers think you are? a) very b) not bad, could be better c) not at all	
7	How do you react when someone interrupts you? a) you feel annoyed, but try to be helpful b) you are happy to oblige c) you tell them that you are busy, and suggest that they find someone else to help them	
8	How would your contacts describe your listening skills? a) excellent b) all right at times c) poor	

	Question	ABC
9	How often do you smile while talking on the telephone? a) usually b) sometimes c) why bother – the caller can't see me	
10	What is the first thing you say when someone calls? a) telephone number b) your/company name c) good morning/afternoon	
11	Do you thank the caller at the end of the call? a) always b) sometimes c) only if they have been nice	
12	How would you describe your tone of voice? a) flat b) open and friendly c) clear and loud	

Score Sheet

	Question	ABC
13	How many times is the telephone left to ring before being answered? a) as few as possible b) four or fewer c) no more than five rings	
14	If a caller or someone who you have called has been helpful how often do you acknowledge this? a) usually b) sometimes c) rarely	
15	If someone telephones asking for information and you are not sure of the answer, what would you do? a) tell them what you think the correct information is b) tell them that you do not know and ask them to hold on while you find out c) tell them that you are not sure, take details and arrange to call them back with the correct information, and agree a time	

Question	A	B	C
1	3	2	1
2	3	2	1
3	1	2	3
4	2	1	3
5	1	2	3
6	3	2	1
7	2	3	1
8	3	2	1
9	3	2	1
10	1	2	3
11	3	2	1
12	1	3	2
13	2	3	1
14	3	2	1
15	1	2	3

How Did You Score?

44–46

Excellent You have a very positive approach to using the telephone, and appear to get on well with almost everyone. There may be some room for improvement, examine your results in detail and see where your scores were lowest to get some indication of where your weaknesses lie.

40–43

Good Most of the time you seem to care about your callers. However, you could be a little more positive in your approach. Keep working at it and try to stamp out your bad habits. Do not settle for being good when you could be excellent.

35–39

Quite good You may need to develop your self confidence and believe in yourself a little bit more. Positive thinking will help you to become more assured when dealing with people on the telephone.

30–34

Need to improve You are too ready to react to situations rather than respond and take control. Take the initiative and be more positive and helpful when answering calls as well as when making them. Look at the areas where you scored lowest and concentrate on improving. Perhaps your self-confidence when using the telephone needs to be built up. The practical improvement ideas later in this book will be useful.

Less than 30

All areas need improvement You are not responding well to the demands that the telephone is placing upon you. Do you feel out of control? Compare your answers with the ideal answers in the questionnaire and start to think about how you can improve. Read this book carefully and set yourself realistic weekly targets. For example, decide that you will answer the telephone within four rings for the next week.

How Do You Feel About Receiving Calls?

Office life can be hectic enough and a constantly ringing telephone can be an unwanted interruption in your working day. But however busy you are, do take a positive approach towards yourself and your telephone contacts. A telephone conversation actually requires more concentration than a face-to-face meeting because you are deprived of all of the other key sources of information such as the person's facial expression. No matter how inconvenient, devote your full attention to the person on the other end of the line and do not be tempted to use the time spent on the telephone to do something else, such as writing a letter, going through paperwork or having a conversation with someone else.

Think about how you are being perceived by the people who talk to you on the telephone. This type of assessment shows you the standards that you should be aiming to achieve.

Read the list of statements in the table (right) and rate your own performance in the areas outlined according to the system in the scoring table below.

...You should aim to pick the phone up within four rings...

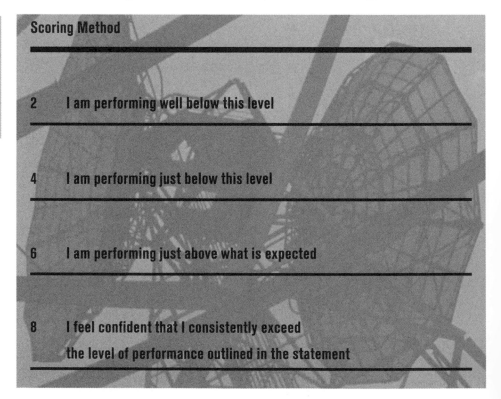

Scoring Method

2   I am performing well below this level

4   I am performing just below this level

6   I am performing just above what is expected

8   I feel confident that I consistently exceed
     the level of performance outlined in the statement

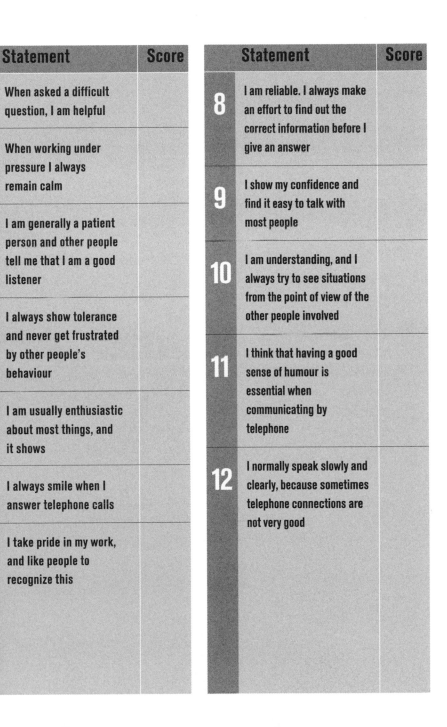

	Statement	Score
1	When asked a difficult question, I am helpful	
2	When working under pressure I always remain calm	
3	I am generally a patient person and other people tell me that I am a good listener	
4	I always show tolerance and never get frustrated by other people's behaviour	
5	I am usually enthusiastic about most things, and it shows	
6	I always smile when I answer telephone calls	
7	I take pride in my work, and like people to recognize this	

	Statement	Score
8	I am reliable. I always make an effort to find out the correct information before I give an answer	
9	I show my confidence and find it easy to talk with most people	
10	I am understanding, and I always try to see situations from the point of view of the other people involved	
11	I think that having a good sense of humour is essential when communicating by telephone	
12	I normally speak slowly and clearly, because sometimes telephone connections are not very good	

How Do You Feel About Receiving Calls?

	Question	Score
13	I usually respond in a positive manner, even if the other person starts the conversation negatively	
14	I appreciate people who are co-operative and I tell them so	
15	I believe that there are always two sides to an argument and it is important to be able to recognize and handle this	
16	If someone feels that they have been let down, I can usually calm them down and come up with a solution	
17	My tone of voice is courteous, even when I talk to people who I don't like	

	Question	Score
18	I am always prepared to take responsibility for telephone calls, even if they are about difficult issues	
19	I usually work well with other people, and I am generally thought of as supportive and thoughtful	
20	Feedback is an essential part of working with others, and I accept this with an open mind	
21	Working in a team means give and take and I recognize this when taking calls for other people	
22	I realize that every call counts, and that I am representing my company whenever I speak to someone on the telephone	

How Did You Score?

140-160

Excellent You have a very positive approach to using the telephone, and appear to get on well with almost everyone. There may be some room for improvement, examine your results in detail and see where your scores were lowest to get some indication of where your weaknesses lie.

102–138

Good Most of the time you seem to care about your callers, however you could be a little more positive in your approach. Keep working at it and try to stamp out your bad habits. Do not settle for being good when you could be excellent.

82–100

Quite good You may need to develop your self confidence and believe in yourself a little bit more. Positive thinking will help you to become more assured when dealing with people on the telephone.

52-80

Need to improve You are too ready to react to situations rather than taking control. Take the initiative and be more positive and helpful when answering calls as well as when making them. Look at the areas where you scored lowest and concentrate on improving them. Perhaps your self-confidence when using the telephone needs to be built up. The practical improvement ideas later in this book will be useful.

40-50

All areas need improvement You are not responding well to the demands that the telephone is placing upon you. Do you feel out of control? Compare your answers with the ideal answers in the questionnaire and start to think about how you can improve. Read this book carefully and set yourself realistic weekly targets. For example, decide to smile whenever the telephone rings, no matter how busy you are.

How Assertive Are You On The Telephone?

Being assertive does not mean bullying other people and forcing your opinions onto them. It means giving equal weighting to your own opinions and those of others and being aware that both parties have rights. Respect other people's rights – for example the right to finish what they are saying without interruption – but take steps to ensure that your own rights are also respected.

If you communicate on a calm, adult level, anxiety is reduced, both parties feel good, each is aware of the other's feelings and is able to see both sides of the story. Assertiveness is about behaving in a confident, calm and reassuring way that helps you to control the situation. It is important that the caller feels that they can trust you, and that you will do what you say.

Many people automatically discount their own feelings, or become emotional

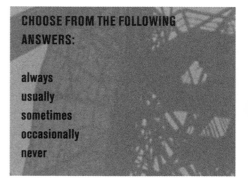

CHOOSE FROM THE FOLLOWING ANSWERS:

always
usually
sometimes
occasionally
never

and defensive when they feel that they have lost control of a situation. By being assertive on the telephone you will save time and feel more in control which should help you to feel positive towards your caller, even under difficult circumstances.

The statements given in the table give you an idea of what you should be aiming for, but do try to give an honest answer so that you get a realistic picture of where you need to concentrate your efforts to improve.

Question	always	usually	sometimes	occasionally	never
1 When I have to ask other people to do things I do so without feeling guilty or anxious					
2 When someone on the telephone asks me to do something I can't do, I say "no" without feeling guilty or anxious					
3 I am comfortable when asking a colleague or business contact for help or a favour					
4 I am always aware that a telephone contact only has my voice to deal with, and I communicate with this in mind					
5 When I experience powerful feelings, such as anger, frustration or disappointment, I am able to control them					
6 When I express anger, I do so without blaming others for making me cross					
7 I say something complimentary when someone has been especially helpful					
8 When I make a call and I have been passed round from one department to another, I inform someone of my dissatisfaction					
9 I feel positive towards the people who I talk to on the telephone even when the subject matter is difficult					
10 When discussing issues, I give my own opinions as much credit as those of the other person, and do not label them as "stupid, irrational, ridiculous" or some other similar term					

How Assertive Are You On The Telephone?

	Question	always	usually	sometimes	occasionally	never
11	When I make a mistake, or give incorrect information, I will acknowledge this and apologize if appropriate					
12	I will tell others if their behaviour creates a problem for me					
13	I give information in a positive way, with positive words					
14	When discussing issues, I do so without labelling the opinions of others as "stupid, irrational, ridiculous" or some other similar term					
15	When I leave a message for someone, I expect that message to be returned promptly					
16	I always keep the promises I make to a caller					
17	I believe my needs are as important as those of others, and I am entitled to have my needs satisfied					
18	I always behave in a positive way, even if my caller's mood is provocative					

Answers			
Always	5 points	Usually	4 points
Sometimes	3 points	Occasionally	2 points
Never	1 point		

How Did You Score?

80 or Higher

Excellent You have a consistently assertive philosophy and probably handle most situations well. However, everything can be improved. Analyse the pattern of your scores and assess where your performance is weakest and try to bring it into line with your otherwise high standards.

56–79

Good You have a fairly assertive outlook, but there may be situations in which you could improve your techniques. Analyse the pattern of your scores and assess where your weakest areas are. Be aware of these as the main areas that need improvement when reading the rest of the book.

40–55

Need to improve You seem to be assertive in some situations, but your natural response is to be either unassertive or aggressive. Try implementing some of the assertion techniques highlighted in this book to make you a more confident person on the telephone.

18–39

All areas need improvement You need to be much more assertive with your telephone contacts. Start by concentrating on the areas where your performance is weakest and put some practical steps for improvement into action straight away. For example, set yourself a target of not making any promises that you will be unable to keep. Assess your progress on a weekly basis.

How Well Do You Listen?

Listening is a skill that is essential for effective communication on the telephone. However, it is a skill that is often taken for granted and neglected, usually because it is confused with hearing. Listening, however, involves not only the sense of hearing but also active techniques and skills which demonstrate to the person who is talking that listening is taking place and serve to make the whole exchange of information more effective.

If you do not listen to what the other person has to say, you will miss out on crucial pieces of information. Make appropriate noises to confirm that you are still paying attention – "yes" and "I understand". These verbal cues replace the visual signals that you use when communicating face-to-face with someone. It is particularly important to make sure that the caller knows that you are paying attention if he or she is calling to make a complaint or to explain a problem, or if you are taking a message for someone else.

Make the caller feel involved. Use the caller's name, ask open questions (what,

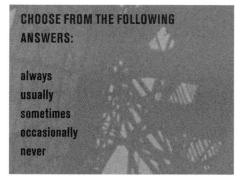

CHOOSE FROM THE FOLLOWING ANSWERS:

always
usually
sometimes
occasionally
never

where, how, which, when and who) to encourage them. Write down what the caller is saying and check that you have got it right by paraphrasing and repeating. This confirms to the caller that you have understood what they have said. Make sure that you find out what the caller really wants by listening not only to what is being said but also to the way that it is being said.

Creating the right environment

Distractions around your desk can be a problem when you are trying to pay attention to a call. Try to minimize them, perhaps by arranging to call back at a quieter time or by turning your chair to face the wall.

...It's important for your customers to feel heard...

	Question	always	usually	sometimes	occasionally	never
1	I always show interest in the person who is speaking					
2	I continue to listen even if the subject becomes boring					
3	I'm able to concentrate even when the subject becomes complex					
4	I try to create the right environment for listening					
5	I listen even when I have no knowledge of the subject					
6	I clarify points to make sure that I understand					
7	I regularly summarize key points					
8	I always give my full attention to the speaker					
9	I always show interest in the subject under discussion					
10	I always manage to control my emotions					

How Well Do You Listen?

	Question	always	usually	sometimes	occasionally	never
11	I always jot down the key points of the conversation while it takes place					
12	I keep a note of the time and date of all my calls					
13	I always get the caller's name at the beginning of the call					
14	If the office is busy I face a wall to avoid distraction					
15	If the call is at an inconvenient time, I arrange to call back					
16	I read between the lines – listening to what is not said as well as what is					
17	I don't interrupt when the other person is speaking					
18	I try to give the caller my full attention when they are talking, rather than planning what I will say next					
19	I always clarify the meaning of words or technical terms that I don't understand					
20	I make continuity noises, such as "yes" or "OK" to show that I am listening					

How Did You Score?

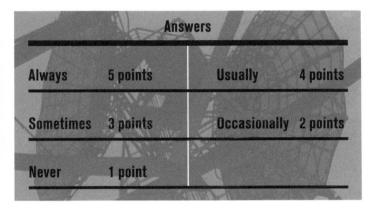

Answers			
Always	5 points	Usually	4 points
Sometimes	3 points	Occasionally	2 points
Never	1 point		

80-100

Excellent You have a very positive approach to using the telephone, and appear to listen carefully and to get on well with almost everyone. There may be some room for improvement. Examine your results in detail and see where your scores were lowest to get some indication of where your weaknesses lie.

61-79

Good You seem to care about your callers, but you could be a little more positive in your approach. Keep working at it and try to stamp out your bad habits. Do not settle for being good when you could be excellent.

46-60

Quite good You may need to develop your listening skills a little bit more. Look at the areas where you scored least and try to improve these areas.

36-45

Need to improve You are sometimes a good listener, but at other times your caller could feel that you are not paying attention and you could be missing essential pieces of information. Look at the areas where you scored lowest and concentrate on improving. The practical improvement ideas later in this book will be useful.

20-35

All areas need improvement You are not paying attention to the people who you deal with on the telephone, perhaps because you are trying to do too many things at once. Take control and devote the time spent on the telephone to the person on the other end of the line. Compare your answers with the ideal answers in the questionnaire and start to think about how you can improve. Set yourself realistic weekly targets.

Taking And Leaving Messages

Perhaps the most important job that you will have to do on the telephone is take a message for a colleague. The impression that you leave with both the caller and your workmate are important. A common mistake when taking messages is to fail to write down all of the information that the person who receives the message will need. Even if the caller doesn't volunteer the information, make it your responsibility to get their name and number as a matter of course and anything else that you would want to know if the message was for you. Although you may not have time to deal with the problem or query, as soon as you pick up the telephone it becomes your responsibility to get the message to the person that it was intended for. If you have to leave a note on their desk, check later in the day to make sure that it was picked up, and not lost under a pile of paper or knocked onto the floor.

	Question	ABC
1	How would you describe your reliability when passing on messages to colleagues? a) I am meticulous and make it a rule to do it immediately b) I occasionally forget if I'm busy c) I often forget	
2	When passing on a message to a colleague, are you a) Polite and clear b) Irritated c) I just write it down for them	
3	Do you remember all the details of the message? a) Rarely. I am too busy with my own work to remember the details b) Usually. I have a very good memory c) I keep a pad handy to write down messages	

	Question	ABC
4	If the caller forgets to give their details what do you do? a) Ask them politely for their name and number b) Wait until they hang up and dial 1471 c) If it was important they would tell me	
5	How would you describe your manner when taking messages for others? a) I am brisk and tend to rush the caller b) I allow the caller to relate the message however long it takes c) I only hurry them if I am very busy	
6	How do you think that you deal with messages ? a) I am helpful to the caller and the recipient of the message b) I am unhelpful to both c) I am helpful to the caller but I don't think about the recipient	

	Question	ABC
7	How do you feel about leaving messages on answerphones or voicemail machines? a) Nervous and flustered b) I don't leave messages c) I don't mind	
8	Do you speak clearly when leaving messages on machines? a) I always make sure that my voice is clear and loud b) I don't notice c) People say that I tend to mumble when I leave messages	
9	When leaving messages with other people are you... a) Always polite and clear about what you want to say b) In a hurry to get it over and done with c) Sometimes irritable and rude	

Score Sheet

	Question	ABC
10	When you leave a message for someone and they don't call you back, what is your reaction? a) I assume that they don't want to talk to me b) I assume they have not received my message, so I call again c) I wait patiently for their call because they are probably still busy	
11	Do you leave your name and contact number when you leave a message for someone? a) I often forget unless they ask for them b) Usually, if it is important c) I always leave my details and a time when I will be available to take a call	
12	Do your messages encourage people to call you back? a) Yes. My calls are always returned b) I usually get my calls returned c) I rarely get called back	

Question	A	B	C
1	3	2	1
2	3	1	2
3	1	2	3
4	3	2	1
5	1	3	2
6	3	1	2
7	2	1	3
8	3	2	1
9	3	2	1
10	2	1	3
11	1	2	3
12	3	2	1

How Did You Score?

30-36

Well done! You are very confident and polite when dealing with messages. To make sure that you keep up your high standards go over the techniques that you use regularly and make sure that you are not slipping. You are an asset to your colleagues and organization.

24-30

You have a fairly good telephone manner, people feel comfortable leaving messages with you and your calls should usually be returned. There may be situations in which you could improve your techniques. Analyse the pattern of your scores and assess where your weakest areas are. Be aware of these as the main areas that need improvement when reading the rest of this book.

18-24

You need to improve your techniques when dealing with messages. Always try to be clear and concise. If you have a problem relaying messages, write them down. If you need to leave a message, write down the key points before you even pick up the telephone.

12-18

You need to really concentrate on improving the way you leave and receive messages. You could be losing business and friends so be careful. If you have difficulty remembering the techniques given in the book, write down the main points to remember and attach them to your telephone so that you are reminded every time you use it. Take action straight away. Set yourself an easily achievable target, such as writing down every message that you take for someone for the next month.

3

Sounding good

Listening skills

Coping with stress

20 golden rules

Do you project a professional image?

Are you listening actively?

Is stress affecting your performance?

Talking On The Telephone

You need to create a professional image, but also allow your personality to show. This can be hampered by the lack of visual feedback. Most people are unaware of the importance of body language in their day-to-day communication and social interaction. In fact, verbal communication usually accounts for only 7 percent of the total communication process. A large proportion of communication is done via body language.

However, most of your body language is lost on the telephone so you need to make sure that the message that you are giving verbally is positive. The tone of your voice reveals feelings and emotions.

It can reveal your attitude towards the caller. Remember, "it's not what you say, but the way that you say it". Also bear in mind that not all of your body language is lost over the telephone. Although you can't be seen, the person who you are talking to has a mental picture of you. Your physical appearance – your facial expression and your body posture – will alter the way you sound in subtle ways, such as the tone and pitch of your voice, and this information will be picked up by the person on the other end of the line. You need to convey:

■ a positive approach
■ enthusiasm
■ a genuine desire to help
■ a warm and cheerful manner

HOW DO YOU SOUND?
Take a few minutes to list the positive and negative images that you feel you might sometimes project over the telephone.

■ What sort of messenger do you feel you are?

■ How would you describe yourself?

■ If we did a survey of 100 of your customers, what would they say about you?

■ How would they describe your telephone skills?

■ What would they say about your: attitude, approach, and ability?

■ What image do you feel your voice conveys over the telephone?

Some days you may not feel as good as you could – perhaps you feel ill or you have had an argument with someone. It can all come through to the person you are speaking to. In a face-to-face situation we convey so much by just the look on our faces. But on the telephone you can only be judged by the way you sound. So if you want to be taken positively you must sound that way. Look at the list of negative words below. Could any of them describe you sometimes? If so, try to replace your negative traits with more positive behaviour. Always be aware of the effects that a negative image has on you as a caller – the things that have a negative effect on you have the same effect on other people. Think about how you want your business contacts to feel after talking to you on the telephone.

A PROFESSIONAL TELEPHONE MANNER

■ prepare carefully what you are going to say and note down your objectives

■ sit upright to avoid constricting your voice

■ speak clearly, pace yourself, keep the tone neutral

■ remember to be polite, and make sure you always leave your contact with a good impression

■ be warm, friendly and consistent

■ choose your words carefully, avoiding any form of ambiguity, jargon or slang expressions

NEGATIVE	POSITIVE
irritable	cheerful
rude	polite
unhelpful	pleasant
patronizing	confident
insensitive	approachable
condescending	calm
sarcastic	reassuring
unpleasant	concerned
bored	empathetic
unapproachable	caring
indifferent	friendly
arrogant	interested
harsh	warm
hesitant	relaxed
abrasive	sensitive
abrupt	sympathetic

Listening On The Telephone

Listening is a skill and can therefore be developed and improved with self-awareness, discipline and practice. Maintaining concentration is one of the main barriers to effective listening and this is particularly acute when listening to someone on the telephone. Because your sense of sight is not being fully utilized it can stray and bombard you with distracting information. How often have you been distracted from a telephone call by something more interesting happening in the office or through a window? If your attention wanders, to help you to stay focused on the caller as a person it may help to sketch the person who you are talking to.

Stop fidgeting

How can you listen to someone effectively when you are fiddling, fidgeting and constantly changing your seating position? Callers will know that you are not giving them your undivided attention. Likewise, tidying papers and rearranging notes are jobs that can wait until after the call.

Assess the meaning behind the words

You have plenty of time to assess the message that the speaker is trying to get across – the average rate of speaking is around 125/150 words per minute, but the rate for listening is 400/500 words per minute, so time is on your side. If the subject is complex, try not to switch off due to your own lack of understanding. Ask questions, where appropriate, trying not to interrupt the speaker too many times as this will spoil the flow. Make a note of any questions that do not need immediate answers and clear them up at a convenient break in conversation. Making notes will also help you to remember what was said after the call.

If you know that you are going to have difficulty in concentrating on what the caller is saying for some reason, assess whether you could reschedule the call for when you are properly prepared or the office has quietened down. If the information is complex, would a fax or letter be a better way of communicating?

Remain focused

Nit-picking and getting bogged down in details or trivial points will only irritate the caller, as will asking questions about another subject. Tune in to what the caller is trying to put across. Effective listeners hear everything that is said, not just the parts that they agree with. In doing this they gain valuable insights as well as the co-operation and respect of the person they are talking to.

Barriers to listening

Barriers to listening happen in many ways. The speaker may have an unusual accent or strange verbal habits and it is important that you try to overcome this particular obstacle with tact and diplomacy. Do not pretend that you have understood, to get you off the hook, as this will only cause problems later. It is much better just to ask the caller to speak more slowly – try to be patient. Remember that the caller could be bringing important and lucrative business to your company.

Keep cool

Sometimes you may have to deal with a caller who is upset and irrational and wants to complain. Listening skills are particularly relevant here. The caller needs to feel that you have really "heard" them. Do not be tempted to get into an argument. Remain neutral and try to offer constructive advice.

In the same way, when it is your turn to make a complaint over the telephone, consider the person on the other end of the line. Try to keep calm – you will get a better response.

In either situation it is important to prevent your emotions from getting in the way. Stay cool and calm and whatever you do, *never* just hang up.

PHYSICAL BARRIERS
Room Temperature
   Too hot/too cold
Air Conditions
   Room too stuffy
Lighting
   Too bright/too dim
View
   From window
Furniture
   Uncomfortable
Noise
   Internal/external

OTHER BARRIERS
Jargon
Technical terms
Accents
Unusual verbal habits
Complexity of information
Speed of delivery
Volume of delivery
Monotone (boring delivery)
Psychological barriers
Anxiety
Frustration
Fear
Status
Prejudice
Background differences
Expectations

Promoting Good Listening Skills

There are a number of practical ways by which you can make your listening more effective. During the conversation, jot down key words as a reminder for later questions. Make a note of what is being said and what is not said (listening "between the lines" is a useful skill to develop).

Try to assess the caller and encourage them to talk. What are their feelings? Do they believe in what they are saying? During this process of assessment, try to stay neutral as emotive responses inhibit listening. You might like to make a note of key points and think about them while the speaker continues.

Hear the message

It is useful to test your understanding occasionally by asking questions or confirming the interpretation of a particular point. Check the meaning of technical terms, especially in an unfamiliar subject. You may want to probe deeper for a fuller explanation. When doing this you should remember to use "open" questions. They are much more effective than a question requiring a simple "yes" or "no" answer.

Making supportive noises and words of encouragement lets the speaker know that you are listening. Gently challenge any ideas you are unhappy with, allowing the speaker time to explain.

Summarize

When the conversation is coming to an end, make sure that you have understood everything correctly by making a quick summary of what was said. Allow the speaker to clarify any ambiguities and ask questions when necessary.

ACTIVE LISTENING

L Look Interested

Create a positive image in the caller's mind of you looking interested.
Maintain an upright and positive body posture.

I Inquire

Ensure you get the whole story by seeking clarification.
Use a variety of questions.
Come to important issues slowly.

S Stick To The Point

Stick to the point by stating your purpose.
Avoid saying "yes, but…"
Be patient and tolerant.
Refocus on the objective where appropriate.

T Test Your Understanding

Make an effort to listen actively by using summaries, both short and long,
always being sure you understand before moving on.

E Evaluate The Message

Assess the information that you get by taking enough time to think
about what is said to you.
Check any apparent anomalies.
Analyse what is said to you.

N Neutralize Your Feelings

You can only listen by staying calm.
Keep an open mind.
Retain your self control.
Suspend your instant judgments.

Stress And The Telephone

The telephone can be a demanding boss. Have you ever had one of those days when the telephone just doesn't stop ringing? Every time you try to do something, off it goes again and every caller seems to be more demanding than the last one. What if every day was like this? For example, if you worked on a customer support desk. The pressures and pace of this type of job would certainly not suit everyone.

Keeping a calm exterior

Although it is essential to stay calm and in control when dealing with a business contact on the telephone, you will need to find some way of venting your frustration once off the phone, preferably in a positive way. When people have to be pleasant on the telephone, perhaps in contradiction to their real feelings, they often display their stress by snappy behaviour towards close colleagues or family members.

Even someone who appears totally calm might not be coping as well as they could. They may be bottling up their stress internally, until one day they just explode, become ill, or quit. For other people frequent periods of absence from work may be a coping mechanism.

Time to relax

When things are busy and you are working under pressure, it is more important than ever that you allow yourself to let off steam. You may think that you are too busy to spare the time, but this is a false economy – in the long run, taking a few minutes to unwind makes you more efficient. If you break the stress cycle, shown opposite, you will stay calm, efficient and in control.

When you feel you are becoming overwhelmed allow yourself ten minutes of relaxation. Choose a method that best suits you and your working environment. First find somewhere quiet where you will not be disturbed. If that is not possible, take your phone off the hook or turn the volume down.

Give yourself a breather

Breathing techniques calm you down and fill your body with vitality-giving oxygen. One method is to breathe in slowly to the count of four, until your lungs are completely full; hold the breath for four counts; then empty your lungs to the count of four. Repeat ten times.

Another effective method for relieving stress is visualization. Just make yourself comfortable, close your eyes and think of a beautiful place where you felt calm and at peace. Try to imagine every detail, even the smell. You might like to put a picture of this place on your desk as a constant reminder of quieter, less stressful times.

Most of us carry our tension in our shoulders, but you can prevent them from knotting up with a simple exercise. Circle each shoulder slowly in one direction five times and then the other, finally circling both shoulders together

five times. Follow this with a big stretch, reaching up with your arms and allowing yourself a big sigh.

These methods are marvellous for dealing with everyday stress, but in many ways we can avoid stress just by looking at a situation in a different way. View the telephone as your tool not your master. The more you allow it to dominate and control your day, the less efficient you will become, and this will have a negative effect on the way you deal with people.

More Interruption

Inefficient Calls

STRESS

Reduced Efficiency

Bad Telephone Manner

Twenty Golden Telephone Rules

Answering the telephone is not a difficult physical task, but using it in a business-like and professional manner is not so straightforward. It is all too easy to believe that other people are causing the problems. Could it be that they are reacting to the way you are dealing with them? Being effective, as well as staying calm and controlled, is quite a demanding task. You might like

1 Be prompt, answer within three or four rings – callers don't like to be kept waiting.

2 If you are going to be away from your telephone for any length of time remember to divert your calls in order that the caller doesn't have to be passed round.

3 Answer with a smile – it comes across in your voice, making you sound friendly and positive.

4 On answering, give a verbal handshake, announcing the company name and department as well as your own name.

5 When making a call, make sure that it is a convenient time for the other person to handle it.

6 Show empathy, build an instant relationship with your caller by using a warm, friendly tone of voice.

7 Establish the needs of your caller immediately by asking "how may I help you?"

8 Use open questions to find out facts and information and also closed questions to clarify and check understanding.

9 If you can, answer the caller's questions promptly and efficiently. If you can't help, tell them what you can do for them.

10 Use continuity noises to show the caller that you are listening. For example, "oh yes", "I see" or "that's right".

to appraise your own ability by considering the following questions. How often do you plan your telephone calls and how effective is your planning? How much time do you waste on the telephone? Are you helpful to callers from overseas? It seems that most of us could do with some help when it comes to using the telephone. A good place to start is with the 20 golden rules.

11 Repeat names, telephone and fax numbers and dates back to the caller to make sure that you have got them right.

12 Make notes, recording all necessary information. It was once said that "a short pencil is far more effective than a long memory".

13 Double check all vital information by reading back, in summary, what you have discussed.

14 Instead of passing callers around from department to department, take the caller's name and telephone number and a brief, but comprehensive, message and reassure them that you will pass their message to the appropriate person and get them to return the call.

15 Give the caller your full attention. Nobody can hold two conversations and retain 100 percent information from both.

16 Keep focused on the subject in hand and do not interrupt the caller with pointless questions.

17 Remember that both people engaged in a call have the right to know who they are talking to.

18 Agree any actions that either party will take.

19 Finish off your call on a positive note. Check that your caller has asked all the questions that they need to, and has all the information that they need.

20 "Sign off" properly. Although circumstances vary, this usually means confirming what will happen as a result of the call and thanking the other person for their time.

Asking The Right Questions

Using effective questioning techniques allows you to get the information that you need. It should also help you to stay in control of the conversation.

When you are confronted with difficult situations, the use of different types of questions will help to diffuse the situation. The different types of questions are: open, specific, closed, alternative choice, leading, and hypothetical.

Open questions

An open question requests information in a way that requires a fuller answer than a simple fact or a "yes" or "no". As a result of asking open questions we should be able to gain enough information to give the caller a solution to a particular problem, or at least be in a better position to offer help.

Examples:

"How may I help you?"

"What information were you given by my colleague when you spoke with him yesterday?"

"Please tell me, what exactly happened and when?"

Specific questions

Specific questions help to clarify points. There are two types of specific questions: those which request a piece of information, and those which simply require a "yes" or "no" answer.

Examples:

"Who was it that you spoke with yesterday?"

"What is your daytime contact number?"

"Mr. Jones, have you received confirmation of our last verbal conversation?"

"Are you always contactable on this telephone number?"

Closed questions

Closed questions will usually produce a "yes" or "no" answer. They can be useful in the closing minutes of a conversation to confirm all the small details and to make sure that you have covered all that you need to.

Examples:

"Have you confirmed this information with my manager?"

"Is there any further information that you need from me at this time?"

Alternative choice questions

This type of question provides alternatives for the caller to choose from. These questions can be useful when dealing with difficult callers. Ask the caller what they would like you to do for them, but provide them the alternatives that also suit you.

Examples:

"I could find out this information for you and telephone you with an answer by the end of the morning, or would you prefer me to fax the information later in the day?"

"Would you like me to get David to call you, or can I help?"

Leading questions

These questions help to speed up interactions. At times we seem to deal with people who find it difficult to make that final decision. Leading questions should help your caller to confirm the information in an easy way.

Examples:

"You would like to receive that information on a monthly basis, then?"

"So would you agree to a delivery on Thursday, if I can get you a discount?"

Hypothetical questions

These questions test for a possible reaction from your contact. When used in a calm, conciliatory tone they can be useful questions to test the water in a conflict situation, where you are trying to suggest a solution.

Examples:

"If we were able to agree to this, how long would it take to set up the system?"

"If you want me to send this information, would you be able to submit details by return?"

OPENING UP

Closed questions can create problems if you use them with an irate caller. An angry caller can only think about the "problem". Because a closed question doesn't require a great deal of thinking time, the caller's mind still holds on to the "problem".

In a situation like this it is essential to use open questions. You are attempting to broaden the view of the caller, allowing them to see what you are trying to achieve for them. Once they can see more than the problem, it is much easier for them to receive the information that you are offering, and it is an excellent opportunity to reach a compromise.

4

Managing calls
Keeping in control
Answering calls
Voicemail

Do you plan your calls?

How much time do you waste?

How good are your listening skills?

Managing Time On The Telephone

The telephone can eat heavily into your time. It is both possible and essential to use the telephone in a time-efficient way. By invoking good principles and practices as a caller, you can gradually educate your regular callers in how to get the best from you without causing you unnecessary frustration or irritation. Your callers will also feel better as they realize that doing business with you over the telephone is a pleasurable and professional experience.

So, what should you do to manage telephone time better?

Managing incoming calls

■ Move incoming calls to outgoing blocks. Interruptions when you are busy are a nuisance. If you are engaged in something, such as a team briefing or writing a complicated report which cannot be interrupted, having someone to field your calls can be more productive. This way you can finish the important tasks and keep all of your calls for outgoing blocks to make at a time that is convenient. Managing your incoming calls and turning them into outgoing calls also helps you to be more prepared. Planning what you need to get out of each call is more productive than "thinking on your feet" and it puts you in a better position to be able to control the call.

■ Brief someone to intercept your calls for you, ask them to make a list of names, times, telephone numbers, the purpose of the call and any comments about the person who left the message – for example, a note letting you know that the caller sounded upset. Make sure that the person taking your messages is clear about what you want them to say to people who you are expecting to call. For example, if you are expecting a call from Mr Brown enquiring about an order, you may want the person fielding your calls to let him know that a delivery has been sent off. Make sure that they have the equipment they need to take down your messages. It is probably a good idea to provide a message pad with enough space for all of the information that you will need. You can then plan these calls into your outgoing call blocks.

■ Help the caller to get to the point by using the techniques of active listening. Try to keep the call on track by finding out as early as possible what the caller's message is. Remember to be polite and courteous, but do not allow the call to become long-winded. You may find that some people are "difficult to get off the phone". In such cases, take responsibility for closing the call.

Making outgoing calls

■ It is more time-effective to keep all of your outgoing calls separate from the rest of your working day. Group your calls. Save up all of your outgoing calls for a convenient time and make them in blocks. To be even more efficient, you could prioritize them so that you make the most important calls first.

■ Make an appointment for an important call so that you and the person you are calling are both well prepared. Call the person's office and if they are unavailable, speak to their secretary or PA or to a member of their team and arrange a convenient time for you to call back. Ask them to put a note in your contact's diary. The other person will then be aware of the importance of your call, if they weren't already, and should make themselves available to deal with it.

■ Arrange to call back. Do not agree to being called back if the person who you need to talk to is out of their office or on another call. Stay in control: if your contact is unavailable, say that you will call back again and find out a convenient time to do so.

■ If your contact is on another call, don't hold. Holding is infuriating and a waste of your precious time. Simply reschedule your call instead for a time when you know the other person will be free to take it.

■ GET TO THE POINT. Avoid long-winded conversations. Some socializing can be important at times, but be as brief as possible. Plan what you need to achieve before each call, and get to the point of the call as quickly as possible. However, always remember to be polite and courteous.

Planning Outgoing Telephone Calls

By planning your outgoing calls before you make them you will be more relaxed and the calls will be more productive, and probably less time consuming too.

Keep your objective in sight

Before making a call, know your objective. Make sure that you are clear about what you want to achieve with this telephone call. Have the purpose at the forefront of your mind and write it down on your notepad before you even begin to dial the number.

Jot your key points down. To make sure you achieve the purpose of your call write a question, statement, or key word that covers each issue you need to discuss and resolve.

Why are you calling?

Tell the other person the purpose of your call by making a clear statement at the beginning. For example, you might say, "Hello John it's Karen here, I'm calling to ask your advice about the recruitment procedures for the new product manager position. Could you answer a few questions for me?" Highlight key points as you go, so that you keep the other person informed at all times.

Summarize your key points and if you have been asking for help or information, finish with a positive "thank you". For example, you may say "Thank you for your help, can I just run through the main points quickly to make sure that I have got them down on paper correctly..."

Plan and prepare in advance

As far as possible you should avoid punctuating your call with comments such as, "I'm not sure, can you hold on a minute while I go and find out", and, "I'll just look up the figures, please hold on a second". Obviously, you can't know everything that might come up during the call, but you must have to hand any extra written information that you may need to refer to during the course of the call, such as memos or figures. If questions are likely to come up that you would not ordinarily be able to answer, talk to the relevant person about them before you make the call, and make sure that you know where they will be when you make the call should you need to contact them again. By thinking through what the aim of the call is before you make it you should be able to prepare fully for any questions or queries that may come up.

Leaving a message

You may not necessarily get through to the person you want to speak to, so prepare what you need to say before you make the call. That way you will leave the most effective message possible.

OUTGOING CALL PLANNER

CALLER:

_____

RECEIVER:

_____

CALL SUBJECT:

_____

CALL OBJECTIVE:

_____

POINTS TO RAISE:

_____

_____

_____

_____

QUESTIONS TO ASK: **RESPONSE/REPLY:**

_____

_____

_____

_____

AGREED ACTION:

_____

TAKEN BY:

_____

ANYTHING ADDITIONAL DISCUSSED:

_____

Checklist

CHECKLIST FOR MAKING A TELEPHONE CALL

Do You Need To Make The Call?
Is the call really necessary?
Would the communication be more effective using some other means such as a fax or letter?
Is the call urgent?
Is the timing right?
Would it be more productive to make the call at some other time?
Is the person you are about to call really the person you need to speak to?

Preparation
Decide who to contact, with a possible alternative at the ready.
Have dialling code, number and extension number to hand.
Plan a list of points to be covered.
Make sure that you have any back-up materials necessary.

Making The Call
State the name of the person you want to talk to.
When they answer, check to make sure it is the right person and department.
If the person you need is unavailable, say you will call back and agree a time.
Keep trying until you finally reach your contact.

Putting The Message Over
State who you are in a positive tone.
Explain the reason for the call.
Go through your call planner, checking to make sure you cover all of the points that you need to.
Check the understanding of your contact and make sure that any action points are agreed by both parties.

Terminating The Call
Say "thank you" and "goodbye" and use the other person's name. Always try to finish on a positive note, making sure that the other party replaces their receiver first.
Make a record of the key points of the conversation, and any actions that you need to take.

Leaving A Message
Have your message prepared in advance. Even if you have arranged the time to make the call, you may not necessarily get through to the person who you want to speak to. You may encounter either a receptionist or an answerphone. Be clear in your mind what message you will leave should you need to.

Avoiding The Run Around

How many times have you tried to get hold of someone by telephone, but when you ask to speak to them you are told that they are not available or on another call. Later in the day, you get a message that "Mr........... has returned your call", so you call back, only to find that he is unavailable again. This frustrating process can go on for days, each person continually returning the other's call, but never actually making contact. STOP THERE! You are playing "telephone tag" and wasting both your own time and that of the person you are trying to get hold of. To stop "telephone tag" before it starts follow some simple rules and leave effective messages.

Leave a comprehensive message

Sometimes you may not actually need to talk to the other person. Think carefully about whether a fax or letter would actually serve your purposes better. If the telephone is the only way, try to get the information that you need by leaving a comprehensive message: "This is Donna Laurie. I'd like Christopher Ledbury to return my call. What I need to know is what days next week he will be available for a consultation. I will only be available on Tuesday morning or Thursday after 3 pm, so if he can arrange

his diary around this we will be able to meet." When Christopher returns the call, even if Donna is unavailable he can leave a message for her stating the information that she required. She then receives the information, and has no need to phone Christopher back, except perhaps to confirm that she has received the message and that the arrangement is suitable – and she can do this via another message if she has to!

When you need to talk

If you really need to speak to your contact, leave a message similar to the following example: "This is Ann Wells, I need to speak with Julian, tell him I'll be in my office, either from 2–4 pm this afternoon. Alternatively, I will be available from 9.30 am until 12.30 pm tomorrow. I would appreciate it if he would call me so that we can discuss the project that we are working on." At once Julian knows what the call is about so he can prepare himself, and the time slots mean that he can organize his time so that he calls back when Ann is there.

Leaving an effective message ensures that you make contact with your client in the shortest possible time. Besides saving you precious time, it cuts down on telephone bills. Time invested in learning this simple process is time well spent.

Answering The Telephone

WASTED TELEPHONE TIME

Research has shown that 21 percent of all time spent on the telephone in business is wasted, and time means money. Priority Management, a time-management consultancy, carried out research into the time wasted on the telephone and said that 55 percent of all calls received by executives are less important than the work they have interrupted. So an excellent way of using time more effectively is to finish the important jobs in hand and then return the calls you need to on a priority basis. Have the calls that you don't need to deal with personally handled by someone else.

The moment you pick up a ringing telephone in your office you instantly become the most important person in your organization. It does not matter who you are – the post boy or the managing director – to the person making the call you *are* the organization, so it is essential that what they hear and the mental picture that they build from that is a positive one.

It does not matter who is calling. Even if it is a wrong number, a rude response will leave a bad impression of your company and who knows, in the future this could mean the difference between making a sale or losing business.

When answering a call, you should aim to do more than convey a good professional approach and image – you should be letting your personality come through. Behave in a way that you know will project the best impression, not only of you as an individual, but also of the organization you represent. If you do this effectively, it is likely to influence the behaviour of the caller, resulting in efficient and confident call handling.

The first 30 seconds count

Getting the call off to the best possible start is a crucial element in being able to direct the flow of the call and stay in control. Try to answer the call as quickly as possible, but do not pick up the receiver until you are ready and concentrating on the call. It is very rude and disconcerting for the person at the other end of the line if the receiver is picked up and there follows a dreadful silence, or worse, the sound of laughter or another conversation going on in the background.

Greeting the caller

You are aiming to make the caller pleased that he or she chose to do business with you or your company. You are aiming to impress the caller with your knowledge, ability, helpfulness and courtesy. So answer the telephone with a smile and let the caller know immediately who they are dealing with. "Good morning, sales department, Chris speaking, how may I help you?" This is known as giving a verbal handshake. This method of answering the telephone lets the caller know that they have your full attention and that you are pleased that they have rung.

Body language does matter

Even though the caller cannot see you, your body language is still important. On the telephone your voice can convey a lot of information about your general demeanour. It will automatically mirror your facial expression. The caller will be able to "hear" a frown. In a similar way your tone of voice will be affected by your posture, so sit up straight.

Building rapport

Get the caller's name. It is much nicer to speak to a person and address him or her by name, rather than speaking to an anonymous voice. You will find people are much more cooperative when you do this – salesmen have been using the technique for years.

In order to control the call, ask lots of questions beginning with what, when, how, where and who, to draw out the details and identify the purpose of the call. Summarize and clarify the main points throughout the conversation, to make sure that you are both clear about the important details. A little humour does not go amiss, as long as you don't stray off the point too much.

Taking a message

How often have you put the phone down after taking a message, only to realize that you have not got the caller's number? We have all done it, and usually when we are frantically busy with other things. But it illustrates the importance of taking comprehensive messages. The failure to take down a message could, at the very least, lead to frustration and, at worst, lead to the loss of business.

Be prepared: have a pen and a notepad by the phone. There is nothing more unprofessional than scrabbling around for writing utensils while your caller holds the line. To help you take better messages, make up a message pad in advance like the one on page 60.

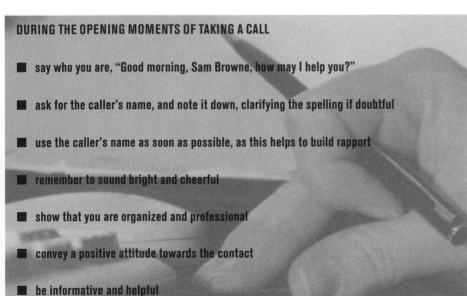

DURING THE OPENING MOMENTS OF TAKING A CALL

- say who you are, "Good morning, Sam Browne, how may I help you?"

- ask for the caller's name, and note it down, clarifying the spelling if doubtful

- use the caller's name as soon as possible, as this helps to build rapport

- remember to sound bright and cheerful

- show that you are organized and professional

- convey a positive attitude towards the contact

- be informative and helpful

Answering The Telephone

Here is a suggested telephone message pad that will help you to eliminate all types of "phone tag".

MESSAGE PAD

Date   Time

Priority
A = URGENT/ B = IMPORTANT/ C = NO ACTION

Message for

Taken by

Caller's name

Phonetic spelling

Company

Tel. No   Extn. No

Message

Caller's mood
(for example, angry/frustrated/good humoured etc.)

Call back

Date   Time

Transferring Calls

It is a great source of annoyance to make a telephone call somewhere and to get the immediate response "You've got through to the wrong person". This answer suggests that the caller is at fault. It is almost like saying, "You have deliberately asked to be put through to the wrong person". So when you receive a call which is not for you or your department be very careful not to give this impression.

Once you have found out from the caller that they have connected with the wrong person, it is important to let them know quickly. Ask the caller their name and find out what help they need. Then tell your caller who you think will be able to help them.

Having identified the correct contact, ask your caller, "Would you like me to transfer you to Mr. Davies, or would you like me to take your telephone number and ask him to call you back?"

If the caller says, "Please transfer me" then put them on hold and call through to Mr. Davies. Tell him, for example, "I have a Ms. Kelley on the telephone, she needs to find out what has happened to the documents that you promised to forward to her when she spoke with you on Thursday, I'll put her through now." Then go back to your caller and say, "I'm putting you through to Mr. Davies now", and transfer the call.

It is also important to explain your holding system. If you don't have "muzak" inform your caller, so that when they hear the silence they don't think that they have been cut off. Also, if it takes you a while to find out who your caller needs to speak to, keep your caller informed of your progress. You might say, for example, "I'm still trying to find Mr. Davies, would you like to hold?"

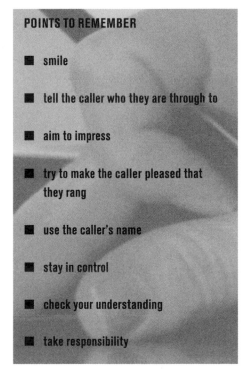

POINTS TO REMEMBER

- smile

- tell the caller who they are through to

- aim to impress

- try to make the caller pleased that they rang

- use the caller's name

- stay in control

- check your understanding

- take responsibility

Voicemail

This is another of those technological innovations designed to help people at work, that has succeeded in generating frustration, irritation and hostile behaviour. Although the invention is brilliant, its implementation and use is often appalling!

In its simplest form, voicemail is a glorified answering machine, yet as popular as answering machines are, many people still hesitate to leave messages. The idea of talking to a machine makes many people feel self-conscious. Yet properly used, an answering machine can be an effective business tool. But most users don't know how to use voicemail to effect, and most organizations don't have a suitable voicemail policy.

What do users do wrong?

How often have you telephoned someone expecting them to be there, only to be put through to their voicemail? The departure from what was expected (a human at the other end of the telephone) immediately takes us aback and, depending on the reason for the call in the first place, will often give rise to irritation or annoyance.

How often have you heard:

"I am in today but away from my desk for the moment, so please leave a message after the tone…"

This is a meaningless statement. If you leave a message, it might be reasonable to expect a return call in, say, half an hour. When your call is not returned, you might call again, only to hear the same message. This time you will probably leave either a disgruntled sounding message or just hang up in frustration.

Another common but vague message is "I'm away from my desk for half an hour, so leave a message after the tone or call back later…" At least a time frame has been given, but the question that this message raises is "half an hour from when? now? 20 minutes ago?"

So, what should you do? Use common sense, think of the person listening to the message and anticipate the reaction your message might provoke. If someone telephones they usually want something that could well be vital to their plans for the rest of the day. Whatever the reason for the call, your message should illuminate and not irritate.

Give specific times in your message:

"This is John Smith's voicemail, on Tuesday 12th May. I will be away from my desk until 11.30 am today, so if you would like to leave a message, please do so after the tone…"

Or give the caller an alternative contact. "This is John Smith's voicemail on Tuesday 12th, I will be out of the office until Wednesday 13th. Either leave a message after the tone or call Pat Roberts on extension 1179…"

Both of the above messages give specific information to help the caller. Although it is frustrating being unable to speak to you there and then, at least the caller will know when you will be available. They can make a realistic choice.

When leaving a message always give your name, an explanation of who you are (if necessary), the day and time of your call, the purpose of the call, and the best time to be called back.

5

Assertiveness
Conflicts
Complaints
Confidence

How assertive are you?

Do you avoid confrontations?

What are your strengths?

Being Assertive In Difficult Situations

Remember the rules of effective communication. Be clear in your own mind and in what you say. Be brief. Concise messages are easier to receive and retain. Empathize, put yourself in the contact's shoes.

...Introduce yourself properly right away...

It is easy to blame bad communication and bad behaviour over the telephone on other people, but we need to take a critical look at ourselves from time to time.

Understanding something about what makes people behave in certain ways and understanding why it is that we react in the way that we do is part of understanding how to use the telephone. When we feel uncertain, or under pressure, we often overreact – afterwards thinking, "I wish I hadn't said that…"

People have different perceptions of what they hear. The barriers to effective listening (see page 41) affect the way we deal with others over the telephone. Also, poor planning by callers often leads to overreactions.

Using the wrong word, phrase or even tone can evoke an extreme reaction from someone who in a face-to-face situation would have been perfectly friendly. So why does the telephone change a person's behaviour patterns? The principal factor is distancing. Some callers feel that from the safety of the telephone they can be as rude as they like. The telephone allows them to vent their feelings or grievances in the comfort of their own territory and they feel empowered by the fact that they are some distance away from the person they are abusing, so there is no chance of a physical fight.

Also, because you can't see the other person, the telephone can have the psychological effect of dehumanizing the interaction – it is a voice at the other end of the line, not a real person. If a caller is being difficult, it is easy to think this and to try to get off the line as soon as possible. But the voice does belong to a real person, someone who also has feelings, and to make positive interactions you need the skills to deal constructively with problem calls in a way that helps you and the caller.

Assertiveness and the telephone

To help a disgruntled caller it is crucial that you keep control. However angry or frustrated the customer might be, he or she wants you to solve the problem.

Be assertive about getting results in a way that you are both happy with. Assertiveness is about achieving equilibrium in the fastest time. If you are communicating on a calm, adult level, then anxiety is reduced and an agreement or compromise can be achieved. Both parties feel good, each person is aware of the other's feelings and so is able to see two sides of the story.

When receiving a call from someone who is unhappy or dissatisfied with something that you have said or done, or something they think you might have said

or done, you must first show them that you have listened to what they have said. The easiest way to let your caller know you are listening is to paraphrase what they have said in a positive, non-judgmental way. Any implied criticism will create a breakdown in communication.

Once you have the caller's attention, you can then tell them what you can do to help. Let your caller know what further action you are prepared to take to help the situation.

Assertiveness is about behaving in a confident, calm and reassuring way that helps you to control the situation. It is important that you do not negate the caller's feelings. The caller must be able to feel that they can trust you, and that you will do what you say.

THREE STEPS TO ASSERTIVENESS

1. Show that you have listened to the other person. Paraphrase what they have said.

2. Say what you think or feel.

3. Say what you would like to happen.

EXAMPLE

"I appreciate that you need this information immediately, unfortunately I am not in a position to give it to you until it has been checked by our accounts department. I will get the information checked within the next hour and fax it to you then."

Being Assertive In Difficult Situations

The psychologist Dr Lyman K. Style said that we spend 80 percent of our waking hours in communication. Of this 80 percent, only 9 percent is spent writing, 16 percent is spent reading and 30 percent is spent speaking, whilst a massive 45 percent is spent listening. This is why it's so important to be an effective, active listener. If we pay lip service to listening and do not hear what is being said, then the communication process breaks down. What sort of listener do you think you are?

Giving unwelcome news

Sometimes you may need to give bad news to someone over the telephone. This will require the utmost tact.

Make the statement brief, with a simple apology, if appropriate

Examples:

"I cannot make it to the meeting."

"I have to cancel our appointment for the 15th."

"Unfortunately Tuesday's delivery will be two hours late."

Acknowledge the caller's feelings and point of view

Examples:

"I appreciate that this might make it difficult for you."

"I'm sorry to let you down at such short notice."

Listen carefully to their response and acknowledge it

Explore solutions or alternatives wherever possible.

Examples:

"I understand that you would like the delivery by 2 pm today. This is not possible, but we can get it to you by 11 am tomorrow."

"I appreciate you are annoyed that we are unable to let you have this information. Unfortunately we are not in a position to help at this stage. However, as soon as we do have all the relevant facts, we will let you have them."

"I am sorry that you are having difficulty with your photocopier. Unfortunately, all our engineers are out on calls at the moment. We will give your case top priority. In the meantime, is there an alternative machine you can use?"

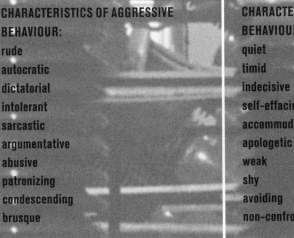

CHARACTERISTICS OF AGGRESSIVE
BEHAVIOUR:
rude
autocratic
dictatorial
intolerant
sarcastic
argumentative
abusive
patronizing
condescending
brusque

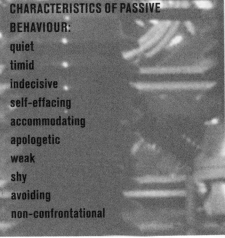

CHARACTERISTICS OF PASSIVE
BEHAVIOUR:
quiet
timid
indecisive
self-effacing
accommodating
apologetic
weak
shy
avoiding
non-confrontational

Assertiveness techniques

There are two techniques – repetition and fogging – that can help you to be more assertive.

Repetition

This technique helps you to stay with your statement or request by using a calm repetitious phrase, in slightly different ways, over and over again. By repeating your request you can maintain a steady position without falling prey to manipulative comment, irrelevant logic or argumentative bait.

Using persistence you can deal with any situation. With the repetition technique up your sleeve, there is no need to rehearse arguments or worry about how you will cope with angry feelings beforehand.

Example:

"I need to have that information before 5 pm today."

"I know you are busy, however I need to have that information by 5 pm today."

"I appreciate what you are saying, however, I must insist that I have that information by 5 pm today."

By the time you have repeated the message three times it should become acceptable to the receiver. It becomes very difficult for someone to ignore you when you calmly repeat what you want to happen. Eventually they have to listen.

Fogging

This is a technique for accepting criticism without becoming defensive or reacting to someone's anger. The first step is to acknowledge that there might be some truth in the criticism. Then respond to the words that are being said, as opposed to the emotion in the tone.

An emotional outburst loses its power when the recipient does not react. It is like throwing a ball in the fog, it's unlikely to reach its target. When someone is very angry about something and they are taking it out on you – "fog". Example:

"I'm sorry that you didn't receive the information today."

"I appreciate that you are angry and I will send the information off to you today."

CHARACTERISTICS OF ASSERTIVENESS:

confidence
positive
approachability
calmness
fairness
flexibility
reasonableness
empathy
control
rationality

Strategies To Cope With Conflict

BEING ASSERTIVE

Assertiveness is all about rights and responsibilities. Being assertive means standing up for your basic human rights, without violating the rights of others.

Feeling angry or emotional can make you less effective on the telephone because you are not able to concentrate on what the caller is saying. But you can cope by using a technique known as "negative feeling assertion". This skill allows you to disclose your feelings with a simple statement, reducing your anxiety and enabling you to relax and take charge of your feelings. Example:

"When you shout at me for not returning your call it makes me feel annoyed because I tried on a number of occasions to contact you, only to be told that you were either in meetings or out of the office. I would appreciate it if you let me explain before you get angry."

Discrepancy assertion

This technique is used in situations where you are receiving contradictory messages. As before, it is important to be as objective as possible, pointing out the known facts without letting emotions cloud the issue.
Example:

"When we spoke earlier we both agreed that Tuesday would be a good day for the team meeting. Now you are saying that Wednesday would be better, I find it difficult when you make changes at the last moment."

Workable compromise

This is important to remember when there is a conflict between your needs and those of someone else. Assertiveness is not about winning: it is about negotiating from an equal position. This means finding a true and workable compromise, which takes the needs of both parties into consideration, giving them equal weight. Compromising on a solution to a difficult situation need not compromise your self-respect.

A PARABLE

An old man and his grandson were standing on the edge of a village, when along came a traveller. "Tell me old man," said the traveller, "what are the people in the next village like?" The old man asked the traveller how he had found the people in the last village. "Not very friendly," replied the traveller. "You will find the people in the next village exactly the same," replied the old man. The traveller thanked him and moved on.

Later that day a second traveller approached the old man and his grandson and asked: "Tell me old man, what are the people in the next village like?" The old man asked this traveller the same question as he had asked the first, but this traveller replied: "Oh, very nice, warm and friendly." So the old man responded: "You will find the people in the next village exactly the same."

After the traveller had thanked him and moved on, the young boy looked at his grandfather and asked: "Grandfather, which of those two men did you lie to?" "Neither," replied the grandfather, "you reap what you sow."

Handling the behaviour of others

Most of our behaviour is learned, and we can make "choices". We know the difference between acceptable behaviour and inappropriate behaviour. What we need to do is recognize what choices we have. When we are faced with a difficult situation the survival instinct takes over, producing a gut reaction to fight or take flight. We tend to either behave in an "aggressive" or "passive" way, even though neither of these types of behaviour is usually very productive. But you can choose to act differently – you can choose to behave assertively.

Dealing with aggression

When people are upset or frustrated they can become angry, abusive, difficult and unreasonable – particularly on the telephone. You need tact and patience to handle both yourself and others in these circumstances. Use all your skills to project sincerity and professionalism.

There are specific interpersonal techniques you can adopt that will allow your caller to vent their feelings and get their anger out of their system and help to calm the situation, leading to either a solution to the problem, or allowing both sides to negotiate in order to come to a compromise.

Using the following techniques will give you the confidence to respond positively in difficult situations.

Listen actively

Concentrate on the caller and listen both to the words that they are using and the emotions behind the words. Allow the caller to vent his or her feelings, without interruption, using phrases such as "yes" or "I see" in a sincere, positive tone to show that you are paying attention.

Then check your understanding by paraphrasing the key points of the caller's complaint or problem in a calm, clear manner.

Acknowledge the person

Show empathy with the caller, try to see it from their point of view. Accept that they have a right to their feelings and acknowledge this. Treat the caller as an individual, with an individual problem, even though you might have heard it all before. Always use positive words. For example, "I will", "we can", "yes", "however", "on the other hand".

A Six-Step Guide To Dealing With Complaints

Dealing with complaints is a common problem people face on the telephone, both within the organization and externally. Recipients of difficult calls almost instinctively adopt defensive behaviour which usually only serves to inflame or exacerbate the situation. Before you know it things have escalated into personalized attacks completely removed from the root of the problem.

Handled constructively, complaints, whilst a major issue for the caller, needn't end up becoming a battle of personalities. There are ways you can diffuse the situation.

Let the caller know you are really listening – recap the main points of the complaint and list the main issues to make sure you have all the information you need. Then you should thank the caller for drawing the complaint to your attention and ask if there is anything else the caller is unhappy about. Throughout the conversation remain calm and make sure that the tone of your voice is neutral, yet confident. Try to sound in control of the situation.

If necessary, apologize and reassure the caller that you will endeavour to find a solution. On no account should you blame the caller for the problem. Treat people with the kind of respect that you would like to be treated with.

As a final check, ask yourself how happy you are with the way you handled the situation, and if you had a similar situation in the future how you would handle that. If you are happy with the way you handled the situation, and you would do the same again, then well done.

But before you get too complacent, read through the six-step guide. It will make you even more effective.

1 Introduction

The objective in this step is to reassure the caller that they are in efficient and sympathetic hands.

Do

Use the caller's name.
Treat the caller as an individual.
Speak clearly, and take your time.
Accept the complaint.
Show empathy for the caller's feelings.
Use a calm and reassuring voice.

Don't

Be abrasive or defensive.
Say "this sort of thing doesn't usually happen".
Ask pointless questions.

Example

"Good afternoon, Mrs. Cole. This is Jane at Morgan's. I'm sorry to hear that your new freezer has arrived with a damaged handle, this must be a great disappointment for you."

2 Ask questions and probe for information

Find out what you need to know about the nature of the complaint, and find out exactly how the caller feels.

Do

Use open questions to ascertain exactly the nature of the complaint.
Give your caller all the time that you feel is needed.
Be responsive to the caller's needs.

Don't

Fire a checklist of questions.
Sound like you are scripted.
Sound rushed and harassed.

Example

Ask the caller, "Exactly how much damage has been done to the handle?"

A Six-Step Guide To Dealing With Complaints

3 Listen, empathize and reflect

At this stage it is important to show the caller that you understand the extent of their situation and that you empathize with their disappointment and maybe even their anger.

Do

Let the caller get it off their chest.
Paraphrase and summarize what the caller has said.
Recap certain key points to show that you have listened actively.
Accept that the caller has the right to feel how they do.

Don't

Say "yes, but…"
Argue, or play down the complaint.
React in a defensive way.
Say, "Oh that is nothing compared to…"
Sound as though you've heard it all before.

Example

"I understand that the handle is completely broken, and after waiting three weeks for the initial delivery you must be really unhappy."

4 Suggest options

Work towards a mutually acceptable solution, something that will satisfy the caller (in order to retain their loyalty) while remaining acceptable to your company. Establish what concessions each party is prepared to make.

Do

Make the proposal tentative at this stage.
Suggest the benefits of your proposal to the caller.
Phrase the suggestion as an open question.

Don't

Quote figures yet.
Put pressure on the caller, try something else instead.
Ask the caller to see it from your point of view.

Example

"How would you feel if one of our representatives calls at your house with a replacement handle, at a time to suit you. If this would be all right, we could arrange a suitable time now. We would also consider suitable compensation for your inconvenience."

5 Reaching agreement

The objective, now you have agreed the kind of concession, is to settle on the lowest value concession, provided it is acceptable to the caller.

Do

Plan the steps in your bargaining procedure.
Start lower, but be prepared to move up.
Continue to acknowledge the caller's right to feel upset.

Don't

Offer maximum concessions right away.
Put pressure on the caller.
Suggest that the caller is being unreasonable (even in your tone of voice).
Give them benefits that are not relevant to them.
Promise anything that you cannot deliver.

Example

"I accept your point of view that a freezer with a damaged door handle is annoying, however going through the process of delivering another freezer may cause you considerable inconvenience. How would you feel about accepting an extended insurance warranty as compensation for the inconvenience that you have suffered?"

6 Agree and confirm

Clarify the details of the agreement and leave the caller feeling good about your professionalism and you.

Do

Check the details with the caller.
Tell them what will happen next.
Invite them to come back to you in the event of any further queries.
Tell them that you are happy that you have been able to resolve the situation.
Leave your caller with a clear picture of what they should do if they have any further questions or queries.
Reinforce the message by repeating your name and letting the caller know how they can contact you in the future.

Don't

Finish the call without confirming the details of your agreement.
Sound as though you are happy to "get them off the line".

Example

"I'm so pleased that we have managed to sort this out. Let me just clarify what we have agreed."

Remember: the solution is in your hands; keep the conversation impersonal; acknowledge the caller's feelings.

Saying "No" Assertively

Sometimes saying "no" is one of the most difficult things to do. At times we feel we are disappointing the caller by saying "no", and so we agree to either do something that we will find difficult, or we say "yes" to an unreasonable request, only to let that person down later on when what we have promised is just not practical. At other times we commit somebody else to doing something that they wouldn't be able to do and that can cause considerable stress.

You are allowed to say no

There are legitimate reasons for saying "no" and if you don't do it – perhaps through fear, a lack of self confidence, or perhaps a lack of understanding of your job and company policies – there can be uncomfortable consequences. For example, time is taken up doing things that really you shouldn't be doing. Not saying "no" can generate added pressure, anxiety and stress.

If you lack the confidence to say no in a reasoned and professional manner, it can lead to a passive, "anything for a quiet life" stance, or to overreact and use tones that will provoke a negative and aggressive·response. Either scenario, will often leave you feeling bad, imagining repercussions, most of which never really occur. Your self-confidence will be dented, as will your ability to deal with similar situations in the future. The end result can be that you take on too much, or you start to feel that every call is a battle of wills.

Accepting limitations

The assertive, confident and professional telephone user accepts the realities of life and the workplace and acknowledges that they will not please everyone. Accept that you can only do so much. As long as that is done well and with a smile, people will accept it, even if they don't really like it, provided you present them with reasons and stay calm.

There are ways that you can say "no", that will be acceptable.

Always explain why you must say no. A "no" by itself is too aggressive. For example say, "I would like to be able to do that for you, but I cannot because I do not have the necessary authority." If possible offer an alternative suggestion, before declining what has been asked. For example say, "Our service engineer calls to your area on Mondays and I can make an appointment for next week, but I cannot book an appointment for you tomorrow."

Show that you understand how the caller will feel at your refusal. For example say, "I know that you won't like this, but I am unable to help you…" Do not forget to get feedback from your customer so that you know they understand why you have to say "no".

Take your time and be patient. Saying "no" often takes longer than saying "yes". People are more likely to argue with a "no". But don't be too apologetic. A simple "I'm sorry, unfortunately I won't be able to do this for you", will suffice. Whatever you do, do not use lies or excuses to get out of saying "no".

Make sure that you do not yield to pressure, always be objective, state what you can do, and reinforce the positive message, only then say what you cannot do. Try to get your caller to accept that you are both on the same side. Use phrases like "we could" rather than "you" and "me".

Words and phrases to avoid

Certain words and phrases have the effect of irritating people or inflaming situations. Whilst the sentiment behind each of the following may be reflective of what we know or really mean, be aware of the fact that they can be perceived as confrontational. Stop and think before you speak, try to use positive phraseology.

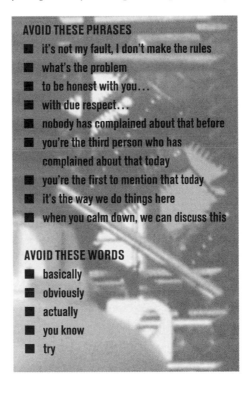

AVOID THESE PHRASES
- it's not my fault, I don't make the rules
- what's the problem
- to be honest with you…
- with due respect…
- nobody has complained about that before
- you're the third person who has complained about that today
- you're the first to mention that today
- it's the way we do things here
- when you calm down, we can discuss this

AVOID THESE WORDS
- basically
- obviously
- actually
- you know
- try

Developing A Confident Approach

Self confidence is based on accepting yourself and recognizing your own knowledge and abilities. Confidence is an image, it's the way that people see and hear us, and if we want to we can project an image of being confident. To build up your confidence there are certain skills and techniques that you can adopt.

Knowledge is power

Become more knowledgeable. Build up knowledge about the job that you do, about the people that you are in contact with, and most importantly about yourself. Knowledge is power. If you know your job function and know that you can handle any questions about it, it's much easier to feel confident.

Be aware of your own skills, abilities and achievements. Take some time to think about yourself and what you give to your job. Affirm what you are good at, and use this as a stepping stone to build your own confidence.

Beware of negative thoughts

Confidence is built on an "I can do" approach. Do not pay attention to your negative thoughts, which tell you that "you can't do it". Imaginary conversations can be quite productive – they give you the chance to experiment to get the right words and sentences for particular situations. Sometimes though, we talk ourselves down.

Your inner voice should be honest, rational, realistic and positive. Recognize your abilities and what you can do to make decisions about the action you should take.

Think of the alternatives. Think of how good you could feel if you thought in a more positive way. Making mistakes is part of the learning process. We all make mistakes. It is only when you are not prepared to recognize or learn that problems arise, so free yourself from the restrictions imposed on you by your own negative thoughts.

In the future whenever a negative thought starts to form, stop it right there. Tell it to "get out of my head". Instead, behave in a way that will enable you to take steps towards building up your level of self confidence.

Value yourself

Be aware of your own ability, recognize and accept yourself. Value your own needs, wants, thoughts and feelings. Trust your feelings as a guide to action. Look back at your previous successes and remember how good you felt.

Accept and enjoy compliments and praise from others and start to give yourself compliments and praise. You can start by recognizing what you have done and using it as a learning experience. Acknowledge all of your achievements and allow yourself to be proud of yourself. Tell yourself what you like about yourself and what you would like to improve on. Every now and then give yourself a pat on the back and tell yourself how GOOD you are. Remember that confidence has to be worked at and nobody else can make you more confident, it has to come from within. Take it slowly, building day by day.

Always tell yourself:
"I can do…"
"Let's give it a try…"
"That sounds good…"
"Let's look at the positive side…"
"We can work this out…"

STOP DOING IT NOW

To develop your self confidence give up self-defeating behaviour such as:

■ putting yourself down, either implicitly or explicitly

■ accepting the criticism of others

■ projecting your lack of self confidence onto others. For example, assuming other people are always right, while you are wrong

■ imagining the worst possible scenario

■ dwelling on past failures

■ having unreasonable expectations of yourself

■ accepting that other people can be wrong, but not giving yourself the same rights

■ seeking confirmation of your lack of confidence from others

■ being unable to accept praise when it is offered

■ being judgmental of your own ability and constantly criticizing your own worth

Dealing With Overseas Calls

If in doubt, ask. It is less embarrassing than completely misunderstanding what the caller has said and ending up doing the wrong thing.

With the ease of telecommunication across the globe you may find yourself increasingly dealing with people from all over the world. This can often mean talking to someone with whom you do not share a first language. As well as straightforward problems of language, cultural differences in the way that you express yourself with speech can lead to misunderstanding.

If someone is making the effort to speak your language, be particularly tolerant and understanding. You need to work harder to ensure that you have fully understood the caller and what they really mean. Hopefully then when you are trying to speak another language, they too will show the same tolerance and take the same trouble to try to understand.

Cultural differences

Often the reality of what is being said is far removed from the perception. When dealing with someone from a different

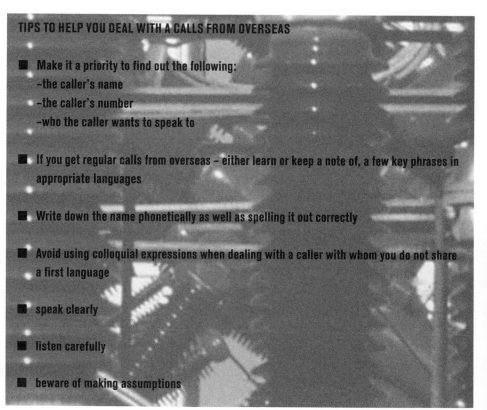

TIPS TO HELP YOU DEAL WITH A CALLS FROM OVERSEAS

■ Make it a priority to find out the following:
  –the caller's name
  –the caller's number
  –who the caller wants to speak to

■ If you get regular calls from overseas – either learn or keep a note of, a few key phrases in appropriate languages

■ Write down the name phonetically as well as spelling it out correctly

■ Avoid using colloquial expressions when dealing with a caller with whom you do not share a first language

■ speak clearly

■ listen carefully

■ beware of making assumptions

culture it is important to try to understand not just what the caller is saying, but the way in which they are expressing themselves.

Even people who share a first language, for example Britons and Americans can have problems with cultural differences in expression. The same words can be used to mean very different things – for example, "pants" are underwear in England, but are trousers in America. Winston Churchill went so far as to say of the British and the Americans, that they are "two people divided by a common language".

Making overseas calls

If you are going to be using a second language it is even more important to be very clear about who you want to talk to and why. Make sure that you plan in advance what you will have to say and make clear notes. If necessary write the phrases that you will need to say phonetically. Try not to be too nervous, practice what you have to say before you make the call.

If you do not get through to the person who you want to speak to immediately, concentrate on getting over the vital information.

- your name
- your number
- who you want to speak to
- where you are calling from

PHONETIC ALPHABET

The phonetic alphabet is an internationally recognized set of words used to clarify unambiguously the sounds of and interpretation of the letters of the alphabet. Whenever you have to take down a message and check the spelling of a word, use the phonetic alphabet to check that you have got it right.

A	ALPHA
B	BRAVO
C	CHARLIE
D	DELTA
E	ECHO
F	FOXTROT
G	GOLF
H	HOTEL
I	INDIA
J	JULIET
K	KILO
L	LIMA
M	MILE
N	NOVEMBER
O	OSCAR
P	PAPA
Q	QUEBEC
R	ROMEO
S	SIERRA
T	TANGO
U	UNIFORM
V	VICTOR
W	WHISKEY
X	X-RAY
Y	YANKEE
Z	ZULU

6

Identify needs
Develop skills
Action plan
Learning

Where do I need to improve?

How can I develop my skills?

Do I need support?

Developing Your Skills

This section enables you to get the most out of the self-assessment carried out in chapter two and helps you plan how to improve your skills. You will identify areas where you should improve your telephone skills, prioritize them and make a personal development plan.

Watch yourself in action

The self-assessment questionnaires in chapter two will have given an indication of how good your current skills are. Try to assess your own performance from day to day and week to week. Each time you use the telephone observe what you do. Record how each call went, evaluate what was good about it and what could have been done better and try to think up a few ideas for improvement. This doesn't have to be a large report. Just jot down a few notes on a piece of paper or in your desk diary.

Where do I need to improve?

Take some time to compile a list of the attributes and qualities that you feel are necessary to achieve effective communication on the telephone. Go back over your list – now put a star by the words that you feel apply to you already. Circle the ones that you feel you need to work on to improve.

Check out your characteristics

On the right are some of the characteristics that you should be aiming to achieve when you are using the telephone in a working situation. How many of them match those starred on your list? People respond in a positive way to others who display these characteristics, so start to incorporate some into your daily pattern of behaviour. You might like to consider actions that will achieve this goal. You will find that the response from your telephone contacts is encouraging.

DESIRABLE CHARACTERISTICS Compare the list below against your list of personal attributes.	ACTIONS TO TAKE In the space provided write how you could achieve these qualities.
■ good listener	
■ empathetic	
■ caring	
■ friendly	
■ approachable	
■ sensitive	
■ efficient	
■ confident	
■ warm	
■ patient	
■ helpful	
■ interested	
■ courteous	
■ enthusiastic	
■ energetic	
■ positive	
■ flexible	
■ firm	

Identify Your Development Needs

Draw up a self-assessment table

In the table given (right), transfer the ratings that you got in the self-assessments in chapter two. Be honest when you complete the list. The exercise will also be more accurate if you get feedback from others – your team, colleagues, your boss or friends. Ask them what they think of the way you use the telephone. Do you ever answer abruptly? Is it difficult to know what kind of mood you are in? What is their mental picture of you when talking to you over the telephone? Are your phone calls efficient? You could try tape-recording telephone calls using an inexpensive gadget, available in most electrical stores. But do remember to get the permission of the other person before you start. They will probably not mind if you let them know that the conversation is being taped for training purposes.

How did you do?

You will probably have identified at least three or four areas where you need to improve your skills: any less than this and either you are an exceptionally accomplished telephone user or perhaps you were not being as honest as you could have been. The next step is to produce a specific action plan that will help you to develop each skill where improvement is necessary. Repeat your assessment regularly – perhaps once every six months.

Skills	Good	Satisfactory	Could be better
Planning a telephone call			
Dealing with complaints			
Managing time spent on the telephone			
Listening on the telephone			
Maintaining concentration			
Keeping calls brief and clear			
Passing on messages			
Keeping the call on track			
Rescheduling calls			
Using questions effectively			
Transferring calls			
Dealing with electronic message machines			
Managing a voicemail system			
Recording effective voicemail messages			
Active listening and questioning of others to confirm understanding			
Talking through problems and getting agreement			

Concentrate Effort Where It Counts

Think about the areas of your job where you need to use the telephone on a regular basis. Are you using the telephone effectively? Do other people find you a pleasant and helpful person to deal with on the telephone? If not, you may be wasting time and resources. Having considered the general strengths and weaknesses in the way you use the telephone, consider one by one the main communication events in which you engage at work.

Focus your attempts to improve on the areas where you are at your weakest or the areas that relate to the most important activities that you do at work. For example, it is unfortunate if you forget where you have agreed to meet your friend for lunch, but if you do not note down an order for a customer correctly this could lead to the loss of future business.

By constructing a communication event list you will be able to consider all of the major communication areas in your working life and analyse your performance in each. Use the example communication event list (below) to consider how you should target your efforts to improve.

Ask yourself what you could do to improve in each area. To check that you have assessed your performance correctly, ask a trusted colleague to check it for you. Can you identify areas where you can take practical steps towards improvement?

COMMUNICATION EVENT LIST

Event	Who do you talk to?	What is the objective of the call?	Is the call successful?
Monthly conference call to New York	My boss and the New York team	To update the team on my progress	Mainly, but I tend to find that at the end of the call I have not said everything that I wanted to
Help request calls	Customers from inside the organization	To support users of my product	Often, but the callers are usually unhelpful and irate and call at very inconvenient moments

Teaching Yourself

Once you have identified the areas in which you wish to develop your telephone skills, you can put together a plan for improvement. Use the model below to consider the way that you learn. Try to make a conscious effort to use the learning circle as often as possible. Review your experiences as often as you can.

The Johari Window

A model that may help you to think through your potential for development more thoroughly is the *Johari Window*. It suggests that there are four main areas of information which you need to consider in order to be able to improve in anything: information known to yourself and others; information not known to others; information known only to others; and information not known (yet).

Information known to yourself and others Perhaps everyone in the office knows that you are the best person to deal with a certain difficult client. Think about why you are the best at particular communication issues. What is it about your approach that helps you to communicate effectively? What do you do that is different to other people?

THE LEARNING CIRCLE

Having an experience

Reviewing the experience

Learning from the experience

Planning the next steps (your development plan)

Teaching Yourself

It is up to you to develop yourself – no-one else will do it, although a good boss may help.

Information not known to others What things do you alone know about yourself? For example, do you feel shy in groups but manage to cover this up when at work by avoiding meetings?

Information known only to others Find out the things that others know about you, but you don't know – your own blind spot. For example, have you ever discovered from someone else that you have a habit you were unaware of – perhaps you scratch your ear or nose whilst you talk. Watching yourself on video can highlight such habits – such as saying "er" at the start of each sentence.

Discovering the blind spot emphasizes the importance of getting feedback, not just from yourself and your boss, but also from your staff and peers. There may be a range of things that you do that affect the team, the individuals in it, and their performance.

Information not known This type of information is the information that no one knows as yet. It can only be revealed through some kind of self-analysis or discovery, which may sound a little psychological and intimidating. It need not be. For example, in your life have you ever discovered that you are good at something you would never even have thought of? Perhaps you took up a hobby through your children and discovered a real talent, or you have found that you enjoy working on computers though you were trained late in your career. These discoveries fall into this category.

You probably already have some ideas about how you work with people, what tasks you do well and what not so well. Is there a pattern behind this? What jobs do you not enjoy? Why do you dislike them? What action can you take to solve the problem?

If you feel intimidated by some people, who are they and why do you feel that way? How can you solve the problem? Thinking carefully about these sorts of issues will probably reveal information about yourself which was previously part of the "unknown at present" area. By analysing your behaviour patterns in this way and trying to find the causes behind them, you begin to gain valuable new insights and are given a fresh approach to tackling your problem areas.

JOHARI WINDOW		
Known to You	Public Knowledge	Secret Knowledge
Not Known to You	Own Blind Spot	Unknown at Present
	Known to Other People	Not Known to Other People

Development Action Plan

Now that you have identified your general development needs, decide what you need to do to improve specific situations and write down what you will do to get better. For example, if you often forget to write down things that you are asked to do over the telephone, you might decide to keep a special notepad next to the phone and perhaps even stick a reminder notice on your telephone.

If you consistently agree to meet targets and objectives which aren't possible, perhaps you might decide that an assertiveness training video is the step that you will take to attempt to improve your ability to say "no" diplomatically.

Select the areas where you need to improve and the steps that you would take to achieve this and photocopy a Development Action Plan for each.

1. Write what the skill is that you need to improve. This may be: "need to be more assertive about saying no to requests for help over the telephone."
2. Outline the steps needed to improve this. For example: "I need to read and adopt more assertiveness strategies from this book."
3. Say whether your boss or organization can help you to improve. If any of the actions you propose would be more effective with support from your boss or the company, include what they could do

to help. For example: "Discuss with my boss how she may have dealt with a problem similar to the ones that I am encountering."
4. Put in a date by when you will have achieved an improvement, or by when you will have completed the target that you have set yourself. You must set a deadline, otherwise all of your good intentions will be left behind.

Try to lay out some benchmarks from which you will be able to judge how far you have improved. Ask yourself, "How will I know if I am improving?" Also consider how you will maintain your higher performance level once you have improved.

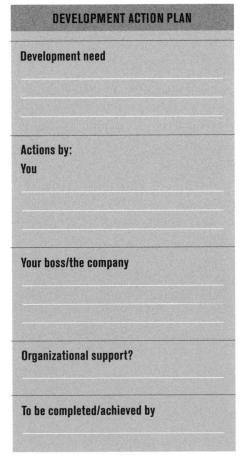

DEVELOPMENT ACTION PLAN

Development need

_____
_____
_____

Actions by:
You

_____
_____
_____

Your boss/the company

_____
_____

Organizational support?

_____

To be completed/achieved by

_____

Get Started Straight Away

Immediate action plan

You may find that the development action plan identifies improvements that may take some months to be effective. To keep you motivated try to achieve something as quickly as possible. Draw up an Immediate Action Plan, using steps taken from your Development Action Plan, or steps that can be achieved immediately. For example,

"remember to smile when answering the telephone" or "write down main points of call in bullet points" can both be implemented straight away. Aim to find at least six areas for quick improvement, including the three given in the example below. You and the rest of your team and the people who you deal with on the telephone will benefit from your improved performance.

IMMEDIATE ACTION PLAN	
STEPS TO TAKE	**NOTES**
■ start improving my telephone techniques as soon as possible by using the formats in this book	
■ group outgoing calls to make them easier to manage	
■ take time off from telephone duty for at least an hour every day	
■	
■	
■	

General Development

This book is an ongoing aid to your development so do not just leave it on the shelf once you have read it. Go back to it on a regular basis to assess how you have improved and where further progress can be made. Development is not a one-off event. The people who do well are those who continuously improve their skills.

Here are a few more suggestions that will help you to develop your abilities, not only in telephone techniques, but in a wide range of business skills.

Role models and mentors

Many people have discovered that finding a role model or mentor can help them to develop their telephone skills effectively. A role model is someone whose behaviour you copy because you admire the way they do things. Your role model may be a successful person whose position you aspire to. Adopting a role model can be an effective tool for self improvement, but there is always a danger of copying poor behaviour. Also, do not forget that you are not a clone – adapt the behaviour of your role model to suit you.

A mentor is someone who works with you to give you support when you need it and to help you find solutions to your problems. A mentor will be in touch with you and will allow you to use their experience applied to your own problems. Having a mentor allows you to access and use the mental assets of a more skilled and experienced person, saving on the time they took to gain their level of knowledge and expertise. Finding a mentor can be one of the most successful forms of self development.

Ways to monitor progress

Working with a colleague or boss can be a useful way to see how your plan for improvement is coming along. Tell them the areas that you are working on and ask them for feedback, see how it matches your expectations.

Revisit the questionnaires in chapter two and do them again to see the changes in your responses. Look at the differences and ask yourself why you have changed.

Notice any positive change in the behaviour of the people you deal with on a regular basis. For example, do they seem less demanding or more polite?

Have you noticed any changes in yourself? Do you feel less stressed? Are you less frustrated with the telephone? Are you more relaxed when dealing with difficult callers?

If you want to improve you will – because wanting to means that you are already half-way there.

Index

Further Development

You may like to develop your telephone skills still further. You can achieve this through ongoing self-assessment, feedback from others, training courses and reading other books. Above all, you must put your ideas and discoveries into practice.

Videos:

Rules of Effective Communication, Video Arts
Power and The Perils of the Telephone, Video Arts
Phone Power, George Walther, Nightingale-Conant

Reading:

Hurst, Bernice, *The Handbook of Communication Skills*, Guild Publishing in association with Kogan Page Ltd., London, 1991.
McMillan, Sandy, *How to be a Better Communicator*, Kogan Page Ltd, London, 1996.
Nash, Tom (Ed) for the Institute of Directors, *Managing Your Messages Effectively*, The Director Publications, London, 1997

Don't delay do it today

Printed and bound by Chorus-France

THE UNIVERSITY OF WINCHESTER

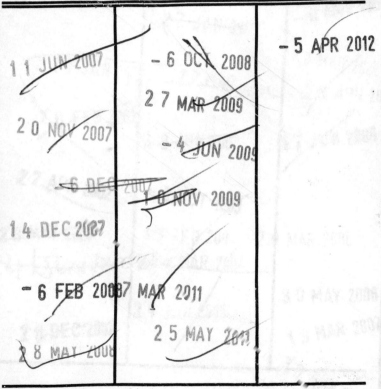